D0606486

THE UNIVERSE

DWARF PLANETS

ABDO
Publishing Company

A Buddy Book **by** Fran Howard

VISIT US AT

www.abdopublishing.com

Published by ABDO Publishing Company, 8000 West 78th Street, Edina, Minnesota 55439.

Printed in the United States.

Editor: Sarah Tieck
Contributing Editor: Michael P. Goecke
Graphic Design: Maria Hosley
Cover Image: Photodisc
Interior Images: Comstock (page 5); John R. Foster / Photo Researchers, Inc. (page 17); NASA (page 21); NASA: Jet Propulsion Laboratory (page 7, 11, 15, 19, 30); Photos.com (page 27); Detlev van Ravenswaay / Photo Reasearchers, Inc. (page 9, 13).

Library of Congress Cataloging-in-Publication Data

Howard, Fran, 1953-
  Dwarf planets / Fran Howard.
      p. cm. — (The universe)
  Includes index.
  ISBN 978-1-59928-926-7
  1. Dwarf planets--Juvenile literature. I. Title.

  QB698.H69 2008
  523.4--dc22
                                        2007027789

Table Of Contents

What Is A Dwarf Planet?

When people look up into the night sky, they can see the moon and the stars. Sometimes, they can even see planets glowing brightly.

There are also many objects that people can't see in the night sky. Some of these objects are dwarf planets.

Ceres, Eris, and Pluto are dwarf planets. They are larger than most space objects. Yet they cannot be seen in Earth's night sky without a powerful telescope.

Our Solar System

Dwarf planets are part of our solar system. A solar system is a single star with many space objects, such as planets, orbiting it. Our sun is the center of our solar system.

Earth is one of eight planets that orbit our sun. Also, scientists have discovered more than 100 moons in our solar system. Some planets have moons, but others do not.

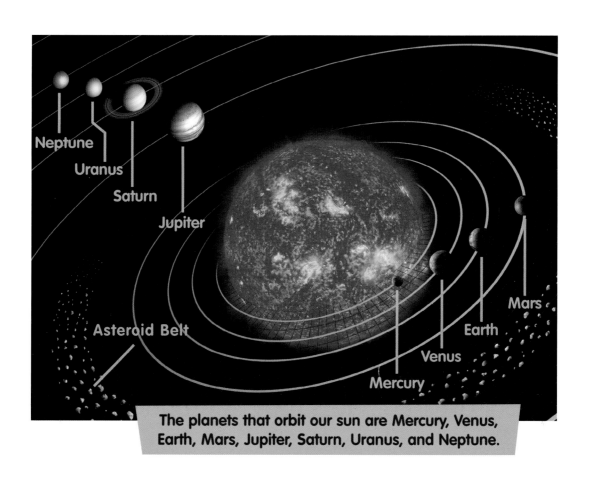

Neptune

Uranus

Saturn

Jupiter

Asteroid Belt

Mars

Earth

Venus

Mercury

The planets that orbit our sun are Mercury, Venus, Earth, Mars, Jupiter, Saturn, Uranus, and Neptune.

In The Neighborhood

Like planets, dwarf planets orbit the sun. But unlike planets, dwarf planets have not yet "cleared their neighborhoods." This means dwarf planets are not large enough to knock other objects out of their own orbits. So, dwarf planets may share their orbits with other space objects.

Like dwarf planets, asteroids are too small to clear their neighborhoods.

A Closer Look

There are three known dwarf planets in our solar system. Ceres is the smallest. Scientists think its surface is covered with craters.

Ceres lies between Mars and Jupiter. Its home is in the asteroid belt.

Ceres is the largest object in the asteroid belt. Scientists plan to send spacecraft, such as satellites, to study it and other space objects.

Pluto is the second-largest known dwarf planet. Scientists believe Pluto's surface is mostly rock and ice.

Pluto's home is in the Kuiper belt. The Kuiper belt is near the edge of our solar system. The belt is beyond the orbit of the planet Neptune.

The Kuiper belt is so far away that no spacecraft has ever been there!

Eris is the largest-known dwarf planet. Scientists believe its surface is mostly rock and ice.

Eris is located at the far edge of our solar system. It is even farther away than Pluto!

Eris

Earth

Ceres

Pluto

All three known dwarf planets are smaller than Earth. Scientists believe there could be at least 11 other dwarf planets.

What Is It Like There?

Some scientists think a thin layer of gases may surround Ceres. They say this **atmosphere** may contain frost.

A thin atmosphere surrounds Pluto, too. This layer of gases changes. When Pluto moves away from the sun, the gases freeze and fall to the ground. When it moves closer to the sun, this ice turns back into gases.

Pluto's thin atmosphere includes a gas called methane. The methane can be seen rising along its horizon.

Eris is a very cold dwarf planet. There, surface temperatures vary from -386 degrees Fahrenheit (-232°C) to -414 degrees Fahrenheit (-248°C). Scientists think that some of the ice on Eris might turn into gases when Eris is closest to the sun.

Like Pluto, Eris is located
in the Kuiper belt.

In The Sky

Like planets, some dwarf planets have moons. Pluto has three moons. Charon is its largest moon. It is about half as big as Pluto. Nix and Hydra are much smaller.

Eris has one moon. The moon's name is Dysnomia. It is much smaller than Eris. Ceres has no known moons.

For many years, scientists thought Pluto had only one moon. Then in 2005, Nix and Hydra were discovered.

Beneath The Surface

Scientists think Ceres may have a rocky center. This center is called the core. Some scientists think an icy mantle covers this core. The mantle layer could contain more freshwater than Earth's surface!

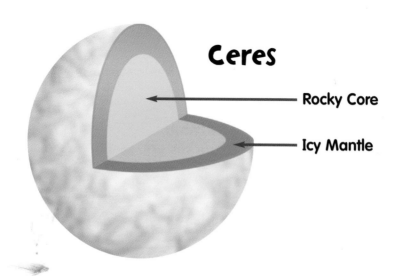

Ceres

Rocky Core

Icy Mantle

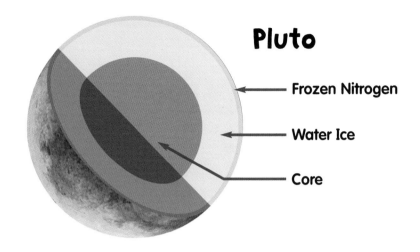

Pluto

Frozen Nitrogen

Water Ice

Core

Scientists think Pluto may have three layers. Pluto's surface layer is mostly a frozen gas called nitrogen. The mantle layer is probably water ice. And Pluto's core is most likely a mix of rocky material and frozen water.

Scientists believe Eris is a mix of rock and ice. Like Earth, all dwarf planets have a hard surface.

Dwarf Planet Discoveries

Scientists have known about Ceres for a long time. Italian scientist Giuseppe Piazzi discovered Ceres on January 1, 1801.

American astronomer Clyde Tombaugh discovered Pluto in 1930. For many years, scientists said Pluto was the ninth planet. But in August 2006, they decided Pluto is actually a dwarf planet.

Clyde Tombaugh photographed Pluto using an astrograph *(right)*. An astrograph is a type of telescope with a camera attached to it.

Scientists discovered Eris in 2005. American astronomer Mike Brown was one of the scientists who discovered Eris. He also discovered its moon, Dysnomia.

Missions To Dwarf Planets

No space **probes** have ever visited the dwarf planets. Scientists have used telescopes to learn much of what they know about dwarf planets. Some of the telescopes are based on Earth. Others are in space.

The *Hubble Space Telescope* is based in space. It orbits Earth outside the planet's **atmosphere**.

In 1994, the *Hubble Space Telescope* photographed Pluto's surface. It captured images of about 85 percent of the dwarf planet.

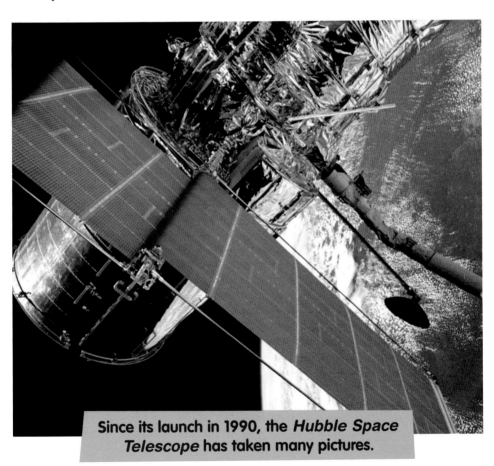

Since its launch in 1990, the *Hubble Space Telescope* has taken many pictures.

Fact Trek

Pluto is about one-fifth the **diameter** of Earth.

Pluto

Earth

Before Eris received an official name, it had nicknames. Some people called it Xena. Others called it Lila.

Like Earth, Pluto has polar ice caps.

The symbol for Ceres is shaped like a **sickle**. It was chosen because Ceres was the goddess of the harvest.

Voyage To Tomorrow

People continue to explore space to learn more about dwarf planets. In 2007, the *Dawn* **spacecraft launched** to explore Ceres and the asteroid belt. These spacecraft are expected to arrive around 2015.

By 2009, the International Space Union expects to **declare** many more dwarf planets.

Future U.S. spacecraft will take images of Pluto, Charon, and Ceres. This will help scientists learn more about these faraway space objects.

Important Words

atmosphere the layer of gases that surrounds space objects, including planets, moons, and stars.

declare to make known officially or formally.

diameter the distance across the middle of an object, such as a circle.

launch to send off with force.

probe a spacecraft that attempts to gather information.

sickle a curved tool used for cutting grass or crops.

spacecraft a vehicle that travels in space.

Web Sites

To learn more about **dwarf planets**, visit ABDO Publishing Company on the World Wide Web. Web sites about **dwarf planets** are featured on our Book Links page. These links are routinely monitored and updated to provide the most current information available.

www.abdopublishing.com

INDEX